Girls
That
Never
Die

Girls
That
Never
Die

Poems

Safia Elhillo

ONE WORLD

NEW YORK

Published in the United States by One World, an imprint of Random
House, a division of Penguin Random House LLC, New York.

ONE WORLD and colophon are registered trademarks of Penguin Random
House LLC.

LIBRARY OF CONGRESS CATALOGING-IN-PUBLICATION DATA
Names: Elhillo, Safia, author.
Title: Girls that never die: poems / by Safia Elhillo.
Description: First Edition. | New York: One World, [2022]
Identifiers: LCCN 2021056603 (print) | LCCN 2021056604 (ebook) |
ISBN 9780593229484 (trade paperback) | ISBN 9780593229491 (ebook)
Subjects: LCGFT: Poetry.
Classification: LCC PS3605.L385 G57 2022 (print) |
LCC PS3605.L385 (ebook) | DDC 811/.6—dc23
LC record available at https://lccn.loc.gov/2021056603
LC ebook record available at https://lccn.loc.gov/2021056604

Printed in Canada on acid-free paper

oneworldlit.com
randomhousebooks.com

2 4 6 8 9 7 5 3 1

First Edition

Book design by Caroline Cunningham

For our younger selves.

For Basma and Awrad, every time.

"I'm hanging out / partying with girls / that never die."

—Ol' Dirty Bastard

" *the one with violets in her lap*

] mostly

] goes astray"

—Sappho, translated by Anne Carson

CONTENTS

Girls
That
Never
Die

FINAL WEEKS, 1990

Hours before, the night outside is black as my grandmother's

hair, its newborn moon in Sagittarius, & in the Maryland

house my mother is twenty-three behind a winning hand of cards

as the water darkens the length of her skirt. December now

& friends still call her العروس, the bride, eleven months married

& the shock of it not yet settled behind her eyes.

∴

Morning & the baby has not come. Milky winter sun

in Sagittarius. I should mention there was a husband, twenty-seven—

I can hardly imagine it, a boy that age, my father.

I cannot picture him in the room, though his work for years to come

will absorb him into countries that smell of blood. Maybe he is

in the room now, not yet a specter. I sketch him in but do not know

where to put him—maybe in the corner, back rigid against

the white wall. I cannot imagine them ever touching. I smudge him out,

correct the still-wet scene. He is outside, long-limbed in a hard

plastic chair. My mother called him *Jack* & this is my only proof

they were in love.

∴

My mother is almost my mother now,
   darker color of the noontime sun.

∴

In the waiting room I should also place my grandparents,
   elegant in that old overformal way of immigrants,
my grandfather's shirt never without a collar, lush neatness
   of the afro against his head. My grandmother could
pass for a film star, hair black & feathered down her back,
   any suggestion of curl or coil since burnt away & set
every morning in hot rollers. Her eyebrows tattooed as they
   have been all my life, blue-black parentheses.
Both of them older than the independent state of the Sudan,
   my grandmother thirteen years its senior,
my grandfather a January child of unknown birthday
   though the colonial offices record it as twenty-six
years before his country is born. They are placid companions,
   their courtship cooled amicably into a sort of siblinghood,
& I have never seen them touch so I cannot imagine it now.
   He paces the cool length of the hallway.

∴

One hour & thirty-nine minutes past noon, that final diluvian
   push & I am outside, full head of wet hair, pomegranate

creature cawing that little animal sound. Pronounced a girl
    & named for a dead great-aunt, the birth certificate dated
& signed in ink. Back home I would have been known by my first
    two names, mine & my father's: Safia Yagoub.
The surname rarely used, but in the new country the paper demands
    a patronym. Anglicized, the ال becomes a looser *el*.
Hilu, meaning sweet, strange unserious allonym of that first
    great-grandfather. & crowded together on a single line,
marked FIRST NAME, our names, mine & his. Safia Yagoub.
    Little echo of that forgotten epithet, that once-loved man,
of *Jack*. & though I am not named for my mother, we match: Safaa,
    noun form of my adjective. Our shared first syllable.
Closest I have ever seen them, him & her, almost touching.

ORPHEUS

Mold blooms on the yogurt, furring the edges
in ancient colors. My body is something I have worn

for other people. Even five years ago
I would not recognize myself today, married, gallon bags

of animal bone and corncobs in the freezer to boil for stock.
I am far away from the cities of my girlhood, cool concrete

of their stairwells. The new therapist wants a list of compliments
I'd give myself on behalf of those who love me,

and all I can come up with is *resourceful*. For a time I believed
myself in love with Orpheus, which only meant I loved

what I could make if I were free from what happened to my body.
That man who would never touch me, kept distant and without danger

by the barriers of fiction. Then I believed the work would save me.
I have no real use now for those Greek myths, their dead girls,

women raped by men and animals. Today the door is locked. Today
nobody is outside. Muscle cramping mid-lap in the dark blue water.

Now I embroider flowers in dim colors in my new country of flowers,
clumsy stitches through the stencil of an orchid, remembering

my younger mouth pressed to a flute, unable to release the breath.
I'd liked that he was a musician, fingers long as spring onions.

As a child I ruined my sweaters, the sleeves tugged down to cover
my hand before touching any doorknob or handling coins.

Teenaged, loitering, urgently lonely. The cotton t-shirts curled
at their sliced hems. Now I am thick-fingered and practical

as my mother and her mother, smell of bleach against ceramic.
Gone is L's humid little apartment, violent stain on the bathroom tile,

a bottle of crimson nail-polish shattered long ago and leaving
streaks like blood. Her dirty living room where I slept

for nights on end, though my own apartment was nearby, cleaner—

PROFANITY

1

i know ninety-nine names
for my god & none for my [   ]

a failing not of my deity but of
my arabic   not the language

itself rather the overeager mosaic
i hoard   i steal   i borrow

from pop songs   & mine
from childhood fluency   i guard

my few swearwords like tinkling
silver anklets   spare & precious

& never nearly enough to muster
a proper arabic anger   proper arabic

9

vulgarity   only a passing spar
always using the names of animals

i am not polite   i am only inarticulate
overproud   of my little arsenal

a stranger blows a wet tobacco kiss
through the window   of my taxi

& i deploy   my meager weapons
[dog]   [pig]   [donkey]

& finally   my crown jewel
i pass my tongue across my teeth

crane my neck about the window
& call   [your mother's   ]

2

now i know the worst profanity
what men use when they need to curse one other
to cut

word i only know as a swear
your mother's   your sister's   mine

in arabic the word hisses
traps the tongue between the teeth
spits

word so similar to an english kiss
turned to venom by inflection
to rot in the mouth

site of shame
birthplace of the profane

but what word can i use to call my own

how   without disgrace
can i name my innocent parts
my wounds

i am saying if asked in arabic
i could not tell you where i open

HOW TO SAY

in the divorce i separate to two piles   books: english   love songs: arabic
my angers   my schooling   my long repeating name   english   english   arabic

i am someone's daughter but i am american born   it shows in my short memory
my ahistoric glamour   my clumsy tongue when i forget the word for [   ] in arabic

i sleep   unbroken dark hours on airplanes home   & dream i've missed my
connecting flight   i dream a new & fluent mouth full of gauzy swathes of arabic

i dream my alternate selves   each with a face borrowed from photographs of
the girl who became my grandmother   brows & body rounded & cursive like arabic

but wake to the usual borderlands   i crowd shining slivers of english to my mouth
iris crocus inlet heron   how dare i love a word without knowing it in arabic

& what even is translation   is immigration   without irony   safia
means *pure*   all my life it's been true   even in my clouded arabic

YASMEEN

i was born   i was planted

at the rupture the root where   land became ocean became land anew

i split from my parallel self i split from   its shape refusing root in my fallow mouth

the girl i also could have been   cleaving my life neatly

& her name / easy / i know the story   & my name / taken from a dead woman

all her life / my mother wanted   to remember / to fill an aperture with

a girl named for a flower   cut jasmine in a bowl

14

whose oil scents all   our longing

our mothers /   our mothers'

petals wrung   wilting

for their perfume   garlands hanging from our necks

TAXONOMY

i go to meet the poem & it will not meet me

so long as i believe i am owed

i call it by the name i learned first شعر

which always sounds to me like شعر

without their vowels they are the same,

the poem & my brother's hair

these days the longest i've seen it since we were children

it curls around his ears & for that sweetness i have no name

though i must still write it down because otherwise i will forget

as i have forgotten so many others

words i mean & also the suffix built in to mark my labors

specter, daughter, agent noun attached to the verb of my origins

a sheet dotted with blood, a thumbprint against the dotted line

& even if i am not tender i must tend

& though i am only part water i wait

& like any number i numb my vulgar parts

the word as i learned it first just means *girl*

my mother's girl, grandmother's grandgirl

garland of egyptian jasmine

we call my grandmother's grandmother *nena*

which might not be her real name but i never thought to ask

& before hers the names for me go silent

& i do not know what to call those women

my great grand others, my agents, my tender nouns

the name i am owed will not meet me

though i fast until the corners of the room crowd with specters

though my body swells with the volumes of this blood,

though i spilled it

though i read that family honor is in the body of the girl, i spilled it

i overflowed & was called a flower

i grew up mapless & was pointed to a maple tree

i shrank my own body until the blood stopped coming

until i dropped my every suffix & woke up to the sheets still white

INFIBULATION STUDY

I will begin by writing a sentence about cutting. I will begin by writing a sentence about silence. I will continue by writing a sentence about cutting. I will proceed to ask the question about cutting. I will proceed from this point without euphemism. The question is about the clitoris. I call my cousins in turn. I ask the question about the clitoris. I will begin by writing a sentence about the clitoris. I will begin with the assumption that we each continue to have a clitoris. False. We do not talk about this. I will begin with speculation about our mothers, that each continues to have a clitoris. False. We are never to ask. In the silence, my youngest cousin asks if our grandmothers were cut. We were meant to proceed without euphemism. The Arabic, however, does not allow it. The Arabic, cut by euphemism. We do not use the word *cut*. The word we use, left intact, is *purified*. I will ask. I will begin. I was born & allowed to mature uncut. I was born with a clitoris & remain uncut. I was born unnamed & upon arrival was given my orders. I was born &

named for a woman who died. The Arabic here allows for nuance. My name, ours, is not the same as the word we use to mean *cut*. That word, conjugated, is the name of one of my grandmothers. I will not ask her the question. I am told she does not remember.

POMEGRANATE

Because I am their daughter my body is not mine.
I was raised like fruit, unpeeled & then peeled. Raised
to bleed in some man's bed. I was given my name
& with it my instructions. Pure. *Pure*.

& is it wasted on me? Every moment I do not touch
myself, every moment I leave my body on its back
to be a wife while I go somewhere above the room.

I return to the soil & search. I know it's there. Buried
shallow, wrapped in rags dark with old & forgotten rust,
their discarded part. Buried without ceremony,
buried like fallen seeds.

I wonder about the trees: Date palms veined
through the fruit with the copper taste of cutting.
Guavas that, when slit, purple dark as raw meat.

I have to wonder, of course, about the blood orange,
about the pomegranate, splayed open, like something
that once was alive & remains.

POMEGRANATE WITH
PARTIAL NUDE

i know my history

the ocean froths over my thighs
so cold i taste metal

three coasts away from the airport road
seven countries from my garden city
& then of course the water
of course its copper taste

pomegranate in my throat
color of all my sisters
color of all the girls i know

their names peeled & sucked
their names spit like seeds from car windows

their names clinging to every lower lip
to every rupture

sun sets on the pomegranate city
& where are my sisters
where have they gone?

INFIBULATION STUDY

what is to border but to cut   say it   say it as you mean

thin membrane dividing   the world & the world of men

a body i can claim &   a body to be forgiven its breach

a body to be sliced like festival lamb   a body named for what it daughters

both of them my blood to clot   both of them my gnarled protest

to my many mothers i only ask   the thin membrane of their girlhoods

when we became the officers of men   students of purity for men wielders of scalpel & sharpened rock

i only ask about the knotting sugar

making slow velvet of our bodies

what is it to border

which ones are for the girls

answer me

who hurt you

who made the first incision

whisperers of spells & prayer & ruined name

to cut away what frightens men

to uproot the fine down of hair

answer me

which knives are for the animals

who drew the first blood

who hurt you

who drew the matching wound

ISHA, NEW YORK CITY

i should want to survive   to outlive

my particular beauties   i should want to survive

long enough to forget   ever wanting to be touched

MEMOIR

In winter I'd pierced my nose & prepared to move to that city to be an artist, & late in the summer I did. Hours of highway then the sudden clog of one-way streets, sweet stink of garbage overflowing in its bins. In the new city I was not marked. I named myself & was believed. I wore blue eyeliner & allowed musicians to court me, parade of free-form dreadlocks & perfect tattered white tees. I met him the day I returned from Cairo, seven in the morning at a diner because my body thought it afternoon, because he never slept.

I lived on the twentieth floor & the wind sounded like crowds of women screaming. For years I loved him & could not keep the secret. I rode the train at any hour in any direction. I broke dawn in stranger's apartments, someone always singing, someone always unearthing a hidden guitar. We slept on each other's floors & never asked. Dollar pizza darkening a paper plate, our bodies crowding the F train, crowding the Lower East Side.

The thrill of a party where no one went home, hours in the park colored by the changing light. The long walk from uptown to the village. We were like children left to govern ourselves, cheap metal blooming green against our skin in the heat, cups of mostly milk & sugar, singed taste of the coffee underneath. I harbored every day the fear that he would die. I held my breath when I passed cemeteries, ladders, any naked, flickering bulb. I pierced six more holes into my ears, tended each summer to a new infection. I wore Doc Martens until my feet bled & never broke them in.

I thought I'd stay forever. I thought we'd all live. More than I wanted to make anything, I wanted to stay alive. More than the thick stink of the summer, our knotted and painted bodies filling the train car with noise. Left alone I'd collapse for days into bed, exhausted but unable to sleep, feeling the ache of my fingernails growing long, my chemicals going sour. I only wanted sleep. I did not want to die. So I left. It was six years to the day, an apartment I'd loved. I escaped, I think, with my life. Because I loved him I look up, every few years, his name to check for an obituary. I tend to my infections, salt water & clean cotton.

There is so much I have forgotten, so much I did not think to record. My shorter hair. Those first moments after waking, my eyes still shut, trying to remember where I'd slept. I look through photographs, our younger faces filling the frame, our bodies always touching. I did not think of it as a time to survive. I thought we'd all still know each other, & that we'd all still be alive, meeting years later to retell the story, exaggerating every detail, the cartilage fully healed. I set the table as if someone else is coming. But I got to the other side. I left everyone behind.

Don't ever go into a room alone with anyone. Even if they're family. Our mothers' first warning & the start & finish of our sexual education: Desire as violence, desire as cause for harm. Turning away from kissing scenes on television & thinking, *you're hurting her.* Older now & still afraid, we kept quiet for years & when the quiet was breached it emerged that we all had been. Lacuna where the word should be, not even a euphemism in its place. All the verbs I know name the doing as undoing. & I work every day to forget the word *virginity*, but without it I don't know how to tell the story. Alone in a room waiting to be touched & hoping it will not hurt. Alone in a room waiting to be hurt & hoping I do not die. Clamping tight around the bruise & tending it. Dirigible animal inside me fleeing, only the allium taste of sweat. Wet to the elbow in sour dishwater beside our faraway mothers, cruel kings of our girlhoods, from whom we thought we wanted freedom, from whom we needed care. Our mothers who were girls before us, afraid before us, raising children into the fear. When I was hurt I cried like a child for my mother, for what she must already have known. & who she could not tell. For what I will not tell her.

ON EID WE SLAUGHTER LAMBS &
I KNOW INTIMATELY THE COLOR

i ride an uber spilling the last of the day's ginger light
driver handsome enough to pull listening sounds as he chats

our talk is casual at its center
but at the edges i taste an old brittleness
memory of something burnt

he circles his mouth to an electronic cigarette
& its vapor braids into the earth & vinegar smell of sweat

you are muslim he tells me
not a question   & i nod
smile at his smoke-dark eyes in the mirror

i count the prayer beads
strung in a necklace from his rearview

ninety-nine & perfect
glossy & unworn

mine are sandalwood
& leave their perfume
when cabling through my fingers

drink? smoke?
he demands an inventory of my wickedness
in the way men of my faith think me immediately theirs
daughter & sister & wife
always a test & never asking my name

in the rippling mirror
my head uncovered
extra button undone from my shirt
i know this exchange & its right answers
a blink & head shaken no

he squints his endless eyes
at a red light he turns
counts what he sees in my face

& the light drips in to share our ride
new vermillion along our bodies

i blink again & measure his disbelief
i am tired in the new dark
& ready to confirm whatever he decides i am

for a moment of quiet
moment to rest

my loosened hair smells of coal
floats over the backseat like smoke

A RUMOR

say i was a girl with more triggers than eyelashes
say every hand on my body that heard no & remained

was a husband to be rid of through a process of paperwork
say like a good muslim girl   say they all were a kind of husband

say the imagination of wedlock was a cure
for the dark & copper taste

say he was a good man he would never   say his listening
gaped like a fasting mouth   say i must not have said no

or say he would have heard it   say if i didn't keep so quiet
they would know what i meant

say it could be heavy & shining like the quivering sadness of fish
say i could not tell my mother   say the doors of my girlhood

were locked tight to keep the hands out   but say they trickled in
through the gaps say i was raised to be untouched

& say i was touched   say everywhere the world enters me
leaves behind a wound   say because i love shame

i am ashamed to have been hurt   say the aching makes a low hum
at the base of my remaining life

say my disgrace becomes my obsession   say i roam for days
at its borders   touch it to my tongue

MODERN SUDANESE POETRY

my husband works his fingers
into the knot muscled against my spine   & my dead
stay dead   my hair a knotted cursive language
my ligature   my grief barely literate   my amulets
knotted around my neck & wrists   my language
my language   cursive & silent   glottal & knotted
& scarring the cheeks of my dead   adorning the hair
of my dead   tallow in their braided hair
i read the books in translation   where is the poem
& circle every word i know   acacia   lupin
sandalwood & ash   they ululate   my dead
they squat like brides   over clay pots of smoke
a yolk suspended in each open eye   & some
in truth are not dead   my dead   & i am who
is lost   who is not counted among the living
the poem is not owed me   i was wed in all the colors
of my dead   the reddening   the borrowed gold
i wrote the poem in translation   i wrote the poem
in the loophole   i wrote the poem in cursive

i snarled it   i picked apart the threads & wove a shroud

i was wed in it   i unfastened   i broke my fast with apricots

furred like the ears of my dead   i looked laterally

for ancestors   i descended left & right   i read the book

in arabic   knew each letter & its sound   & did not

recognize the words for tallow   for ululate   my dead

my languages   my ligatures   smoke in my loosened hair

GIRLS THAT NEVER DIE

a girl   embroidered

a girl   teeth bared   locked inside a photograph

a girl dances to the same coiled song   can never leave

keeps her looks   outlives the other guests

filled up with all her teeth   never returns from the party

is never heard from again   is everywhere

Forgotten But Not Gone

cries into your drink & returns it to you

makes you say her name   salt in the well kills the whole village

BAD GIRL

[a bad girl]   they will spit at my sentencing
but i was not bad at being a girl   i thrilled at it
i excelled at smallness   at smoothness
at epilation by sugar & the folding away of smells
dousing oil into my underarms   my underwear
my cottons bone dry   my every virginity
sweet & rotting   jasmine piled into my lap
i wore every white dress   i was primed to show blood

SELF-PORTRAIT WITHOUT STITCHES

i was hurt   i wasn't   i saw it
on the internet   licked yogurt
from a spoon while the girls
described their blood   hot seizing
the cotton of a sheet   i am speaking
from the cut place   from my other
mouths   do not believe me for i
was never cut   or   i was hurt but
never sewn   or   i wasn't   i want
-ed it   i didn't   i screamed   i didn't
i bit down   i bled   i didn't   i click
through pictures of the girls   moonfaced
thick-cheeked   still fastened   to the
roundness of childhood   consider
the softness of my jaw   my face without
angles   without edges   i covered
i cowered   i didn't   i cried i came to

i click & learn their names   incant them
i learn the names of the stones   the theory
it wasn't me   i think of all the ways
we match   it could have been   it
couldn't   consider the cut place   thick
liquid   of citizenship   spilling from
my many mouths   uncut   my many
uncut mouths

THE ANIMAL

i was a child greedy in my skin hungers   my stomach
churned by festival meat   the lamb in the courtyard

with its necklace of rope   gone & in place of a memory
pools of its blood in the dust   where i played barefoot

with the cousins   wearing the small boys' alallah
for which i cried   until mama habab sent for the tailor

crisp pinstriped jalabiya & its smart striped trouser
i took great care to keep it pristine   & cried on days

it was taken from me to wash   twisting on the line
like my truer body   now i am the farthest

i've ever been & the fabric tears   canopy of fig trees
arranged in place of mothers   i face homeward & feel

once again that i am longing   for my uniform to return

from the water   that i am waiting for the animal i took

care to name   to wake & nuzzle its wet face into my hand
i wake on festival days   & reach for something to wear

& find only that bright chiffon   that irritating clanking of bangles
i wake on festival days to the smells of charring animal

& no one to accompany me to the prayer   no one to look
upon my naked feet   no one to touch me at all

PASTORAL

if we ever again meet i have a story about persimmons
to make you laugh, how i mistook them for tomatoes.
i have a story about bay leaves, plucked from the side
of the road, one forgotten & crisped perfectly, dried
at the bottom of my purse. i want to show the way
california inflects my speaking, california in its frankness,
long seasonless line, clear clauses, the bay & the lake
like parentheses. days like an orange peeled
in that unbroken spiral.

i place inside me figs & nectarines, gnarled tomatoes
of the season, limes split & salted to eat like we did
in childhood, collected as cousins, faces always sticky
with fruit. our parents in forgotten shapes among
their siblings, wearing their first faces, bickering
at the table. the way i tell the story i am outside looking in,
but in the photographs we are indistinguishable,
us children, enormous eyes & unbrushed hair,
a drooping sock, dressed in each other's clothes.

in the memory we are a single organism, our hundred
legs & arms shining with vaseline, our feet the color
of dust, in motion. when we meet again it will be
as strangers, & i will offer my story about persimmons
to show my absent mind, my great forgetting, & i imagine
you are polite as we have all grown up to be, laughing
into the air between us.

THE CAIRO APARTMENTS

The cousins as barefoot children floating out of polished rooms. Together we clattered between floors in each other's jalabiyas, spectacular games of hide & seek, three floors & a roof to search. I can't remember if we made the songs up ourselves, *where is the bride's house? Ali Alloy prayed his prayers boarded the boat worked his labors.* The specter of our adults in the mornings & nights, their strained & hushed voices. Our grandmothers were beautiful & suited to exile. Enormous coifs of blackened hair. Silk scarves only for driving. The eyeliner tattooed, eternal livid stain on the rim of each eyelid, bare faces forgotten in childhood. Our mothers were less glamorous & always tired, always at work, wore bluejeans, cool hands that carried us to our beds at night. I loved exile & the close quarters it afforded us. I loved it enough to stay gone when all the others went home, moved on, unlatched their shuttered houses, beat the carpets & kissed their neighbors & cried. The apartments were emptied. I return to Cairo years later & look for our child-ghosts kicking a ball in the corridors between unfinished buildings. The time Almustafa tripped & opened the skin of his palm on a fallen brick, how I wouldn't look up from my book to see what he was trying to show me, how he wrapped the bloodied hand in a dish towel & pressed down until our mother came home. I cannot find us. I more closely resemble now the young parents that corralled us, creased & shot through with sadness. There will be no children of my own to carry to their waiting beds. & the city that belonged to me has gone, was never mine, I dreamt it, I wrote it down, invented it, made all of it up, everything but the smell of corn roasting sweetly on the street below. The carved wooden shutters. Motes of dust arcing through the light. A workbook splayed before me, strained cursive in the feminine conjugation. Why I didn't look up. He didn't say he was bleeding. The shopkeeper remarks that I look very clean for a Sudanese. Ya samar ya samara. Ya asmar ya asmarani. Upper Nile. Silt color. Who taught you to speak Arabic like that? I don't know where the cousins have gone. I don't know what countries we've settled for. I imagine everyone back home, that they might have been playing for hours without me. My brother still with the faint stripe of a scar down his palm, remembers the stitches were done without anesthesia. The doctor telling jokes to distract him.

ZAMALEK

Late August, what I've always understood
to be deep summer, crisp again in the aftermath

of the heatwave, the fires still burning distant
redwoods, though I am once again wearing

socks & a sweatshirt to sleep. I pull a blanket across my knees
& try to remember the particular scents of all my loved ones:

my grandmother in Chanel No.5 & hair warmed through
to release its curl. Instead I remember the smell of my own hair

burning for years of school photographs, dark sheet of it arranged
around my shoulders. I remember the puffed sleeves & white collar

of the uniforms at the British school where I spent most
days silent, in awe of the Egyptian girls & their glamor,

with my own hair braided into a single thick sausage,
its outward curve against my sweating neck. I am nearly

certain we will never again meet. Those were days
of chicken hearts by the club pool, with the classmate

whose mother was a known actress, their hair reddening
in the sun. I think often these days of Egypt,

dusk blotting the day's heat, sweat cooling & raising the hair
on my arms. & of those girls, the children of the rich,

whom I spent my earliest days orbiting, before returning home
to describe to my grandmother the particulars

of their carpets & plates. I was forbidden from returning
to Noura's house after she was given first a dish to eat,

chicken scallop & french fries thick as my uncles' fingers,
& only when she was finished was I offered her leftovers.

I wonder if she's still alive, if she too is afraid, the night around her
swallowing its handful of degrees in Celsius, while she remembers

an earlier self & the other characters in the story, whether
she remembers me as one of them, whether she as well is wondering

if I am one of the ambient names eaten by this virus that reminds us
of the faces of the forgotten, too late.

I don't know why I remember her tonight, & all those girls,
the sleekness of their uniforms, something always not quite right

about my own. & the one day a year for which I'd burn
for hours beneath a dryer, hurt pink of my scalp, to arrive

with shining curtains of hair for the photograph. In my isolation
my braid grows to new lengths it hasn't seen since childhood.

My skin clears & I tilt my face into the steam of cardamom
floating from the clay cup. Tomorrow I will lose them all again,

those girls, those years, my childhood of uniforms & expatriation.
I have forgotten them already, even tonight,

my memories offering no faces, barely scent. I know only the scents
of my new life, distant smoke gnawing at an ancient tree,

cut apples in the morning. I do not want any of what I've lost.
I want only what I have now, to keep it.

GENEVA

It's 1999 & I remember the school bus in silence except for the song whose lyrics list the names of women, its endless loop that year. In school I track the brief switches into English, enough to overhear about my clothes, my strangeness, testimonies from gym class that I run *"like an African."* By silence I mean that I did not speak the language, a trait that found me in the early countries & remained. & in gym class I tug myself away from the steady rhythm of the group jog, ask my body to *go* & it does, *faster* & it understands my language. What has changed, what is different about the girl in that story? The language of the asking? The language of the body? I say *run* & she unfurls roots, *faster* & she starts to cry. In our group text, Basma says *I grieve most for our younger selves.* That cloistering, that cosmic silence, the belief that if we were told in any detail what we weren't allowed to do, we would take from the details instructions for the doing. Told only, instead, *don't. Never. Good girls don't.* Older now & tending each keloid, everything we allowed to be done to us in silence. To ask for help would be to speak & of course we never spoke. *Go.* See her, running, little bird in full possession of that body. Little animal, *faster,* untouched. Of course I tell the story because I fell. Going too fast &

tripped, shot forward, projectile, a hand put out to brace my pitch. Hot spread of nerves registering the breaking bone. Iodine, gypsum, plaster of Paris. Months later, clean slice through the shell of the cast, & my freed arm, grown used to the weight, floating upward like a balloon, like a hand raised to speak.

TONY SOPRANO'S TENDER MACHISMO

I know him: Three buttons undone
down the baobab chest,
quiet humility of the wisping hairline.

I watch him cup a face in his great paw to kiss a cheek,
exact manners of my first beloved men,
sturdy & brokenhearted as cattle, my uncles,
watches matting the thick hair of their left arms,
brother-aged & fathering into my empty spaces.

My father was gone & into that great room
they poured, big-shouldered boys, hot streak
of anger at each center. I was a child wealthy
in shoulders to climb, swung from arm to heavy arm,
tender booming of my name in that chorus
of approving mouths.

Gifts shining & breakable in their hands:
fairy-science of the music box, tiny chime
of each earring, bracelets narrow & silver
as their silent, injured wives.

I am their smart girl & they are proud.

I watch him, my uncle who is not mine, thirteen years
after the show stops airing, & I love him
like the child forgetting her abdicated father.
He smiles like I delight him. My love justifies
his every crime.

I pretended not to hear how they talked
about bitches & golddiggers,
the news stories with hurt girls naming
their injuries, consensus that they are lying,
that they must have been asking for it.

I am home from college & stepping into
their amber scent of cologne & old sweat,
their wounded animal smell, their every tender misogyny,
for a quick kiss on the crown of my head—

Now their girlfriends are my age, now younger,
& now the news about the famous predator floods the screen

& when one uncle changes the channel & mutters about a setup

I watch the flood take that room of piecemeal fathers

where I've kept them installed for years.

Its debris includes the stories I kept quiet,

everything that was done to me that I will not tell them.

Includes every word tossed about to name women,

how we all thought they didn't mean me.

SUMMER

Summer of failed hairlessness
of clogged follicles inflamed

In the afternoons I ride the bus
thighs newly bare & sticky against the seats

Though I am not allowed, I wear shorts
I am left for hours alone

Light of the computer
blue in my oil-slick face

Summer of danger
Summer of want

My body swells in shapes
I do not understand

I am hungry for touch
& ashamed to be looked at

In the silence I know
something is coming

The blood comes & comes
clasps itself to denim, to sheets

The afternoons are still with heat
humid as a strange man's breath

& when it happened
I watched flies coating old fruit

Metallic layer of bodies,
their frenzied feeding

The long afternoon of my life,
long life, long season of rot

maybe one morning she was a girl & the next a wife

not an action but an exile

to [GIRL] it was done at fourteen

clearing away her dolls in the afternoon

before her husband came home

an imagined girlhood   untouched

a girl running outside   going copper in the sun

imagine nothing is done to her

& instead settled quietly at the borderlands

when i was born (not born) (i was planted)

into a damp alphabet of silences

& i want to ask whose children are children

endless maw of that empty mouth

what to name it   what to name

i call out to whatever made me

& the white moon resumes its quiet swim

SYROS

Roads spiraling upward, whitewash of the houses,
little island in late May. My friends & I descend
in our hundred shades, three airplanes & a ferry
to arrive, our rumpled linen clothes & earnest smells.
Sleepier than the neighboring islands, their nightclubs,
here we rent two tiny creaking cars & flush beneath
every curious stare. We drive over cobblestones older
than my surname, landscape of scrubby trees & bougainvillea.
Stark lapis of the waters, narrow streets crowded
with battered cats, one-eyed & carnivorous. The sea still
clinging to the chill of late spring, too early to ease into summer.
We swim dutifully & emerge shivering, to slippery plates
of cuttlefish, cola in the glass bottle, sweetened with real sugar.
Each hunted in the country we departed, we came to crowd
a shared house, shared perfume of its plumbing, taking turns
in the mornings frying eggs. In loose arrangement on the beach,
we sit mostly in quiet, a book tented over each sleeping face.
& in the town square in the evening, I let my breath go still,
looking up into hundreds of lit windows like stars. I lean into

sun-warmed rock, cooling in the night air, & think in another life I'd be a historian. & then it comes to us, in English, its inflections unfamiliar so I think at first it's Greek. Here, at the opposite end of the world. *Niggers. Niggers.* & it was called to us by children.

TERRA NULLIUS

First a blue room in a quiet house, cooling as the sun sets. Though
they live with her parents this is not my mother's childhood home,
the house old but new to them, bought cheaply from a Greek man
bankrupted by gambling & drink. To be born in the country of my
origins would be to have killed my mother. Suggestion of Cairo,
short miles away & with better hospitals. She shakes her head.
America. I uproot her & she crosses the water.

Nairobi, Cairo, Geneva, Dar-es-salaam. I see the world without
understanding what I am seeing. District of Columbia, Brighton.
First the meeting of two rivers, then a city where they join. I am
old enough to choose a country for myself, but by now I do not
want one.

Now my mother on the far end of a phone line, *I am thinking about
going home.* Thirty years away, & it is still there on the other side.
My cousins trickle back as if answering a summons. A house on a
street named for my third great-grandfather. Children borne under
that watchful eye.

Now a little apartment where my flowers die & I leave them there. I take the pills & every month a simulation of that blood. Nobody's country. It rains & the roof leaks, the ceiling darkens. The forest burns & I know it, that carbon smell, from somewhere else. Then the quiet of the tile, cool ceramic against my back. Then my body in the water displaces the water.

SUDAN, TX

Land of the Blacks, they named my country—
at the driving school my instructor seized the wheel
when I continued to drift into the left lane, not yet taught to regard
the great machine as more of my body. My first years here
I would grow alert, as if called, thinking it was that name I heard
being spoken, of our dark concentration of bodies, only to learn
it is a kind of car, the sedan, blackening the air with exhaust,
waste gases I imagine to be named for the act of depletion,
tired lungs of the car sighing for rest.

I say *they* who named my country & don't know to whom
I refer—British, Ottoman, Egyptian, crossing the threshold
& declaring, *This land. Black.* Everywhere the smell of metal,
known to me only as the copper smell of blood. I did not pass
that test & have since forgotten what I learned, thirty years old
& still unfit to drive, *to drive* as in *to thrust, to plunge*, to learn
the responsibility of great violence. Machine in which I sit
& become a hazard, meaning *danger* but also meaning
chance or *venture* or *fate*.

Its etymologies claim Arabic, al-zahr defined as *chance* or *luck*
though I only know it as *flower*. *The* Arabic which also names
my country, Jumhuriyat al-Sudan: Republic of the Blacks.
In the elevator a woman draws her child closer to her side,
handbag flattening between them, when my brother & I enter
& smile, threatening great violence. I learn of a Sudan in Texas,
population 958, named by its postmaster who never said why,
& without the prefix Bilad, meaning *land of*, the name of the city
is *Blacks*. In the photographs it could be anywhere, long flat stretch
of road, power lines & grass. But I want what I am promised.
Thick cough of exhaust, then the great machine arriving,
my body sighing for rest.

TAXONOMY

because i cannot find the words

because i know only euphemism for my tenderest part

i name that absence of a daughter

in the feminine tense

lacuna   caesura

in the tradition of naming girls for absence

safia   pure

or the grandmothers' grandmothers whose names i never asked

because i cannot find the words

or because i will not speak them

those worlds   i will not speak them

because language coarsens through my teeth

because *demur* lives inside *demure* but inside of *restive* is *rest*

because i want to contain my own solution

i should want as well to dissolve

BORDER/SOFTER

& then how boundless could i make my life
which for all its smallness still exhausts me

balancing act of all my margins all my conjugations
of cannot   if i live through the night i will bleed

into all my edges until i am no longer a stroke
of some careless man's pen   *after*

a particularly liquid lunch [man] was said
to have created [country] with a stroke of his [implement]

& isn't a map only a joke we all agreed into a fact
& where can i touch the equator   & how will i know

i am touching it   & where is the end of my country
the beginning of the next   how will i know i've crossed over

ODE TO MY HOMEGIRLS

smelling of orange rind   of cardamom

   most beautiful girls in the world   *wake up bitch*

      we're getting waffles   *you can keep crying*

but you're going out   my marriages

   my alibis   my bright & hardy stalks

      of protea   & all i know of love i learned

at thirteen   dialing basma's home phone

   by heart   to three-way call whatever boy

      so that weeks later   when the phone bill came

only basma's familiar number beside the time stamp

   clearing my name   basma herself staying awake

      for hours   to hang up the phone after

you who send pictures of your rashes

   to the group text   & long voice notes

      from the bathtub   your laughter echoing against the tiles

you who scatter the world's map   piling into

   cheap buses & budget airlines   four of us asleep

      in my dorm bed   six of us overflowing

my studio apartment   false lashes for weeks after

   like commas in my every pillowcase   you clog my toilet

      & admit it   you text me screenshots

from the gucci fashion show   *getting rich*

   so i can get u this   & when i lived alone

      & that man followed me

one night home from the six train

   up lexington   & into the hallway

      tried for hours to break open my front door

you took turns from all your cities   & stayed

   overnight with me on the phone   for three days

      snoring & murmuring in your sleep

GIRLS THAT NEVER DIE

perhaps a cow
some gold
for a girl

carried kicking from
her father's house

from her father's name
& slung over a shoulder

& passed
to another

whose belonging will name her
will give her form

girl like water
shapeless without the bowl

girl   perhaps cut
perhaps in the pharaonic way
sent off to be split

girl as paintbrush
sent off to stain a sheet

perhaps by cover of night
perhaps the husband is old

& the girl a child
legs clamped tight
as if by stitching

perhaps his brothers
perhaps his cousins

men as ropes
as chains

brought in
to peel the girl like young fruit

the pith still bitter
still clinging to the rind

ELEGY

see her: little cousin, little sister, sparrow-boned, alive.

i want to turn to firewood everything that hurts her.

i do not have the verbs for what i need for her.

i needed them myself & was not protected.

i want to make ash of this world that did not protect us

& from that nourished soil sprout one better.

at the kitchen table we eat a glutinous stew

with our soft hands, submerged to the second knuckle

& she is telling me a story & she is telling it quickly

short chirp of her laugh as she tries to mold from it the joke, the old story of our girlhoods; the ways we haunt

the houses built to keep the world out, to keep us safe;

the ways we still were hurt; the ways we could not tell anyone

what was done to us; the ways we swallowed blame, smooth pebble

in the shut mouth; the ways we could not tell our mothers

when we needed them the most. i see her & i am fourteen,

i am twenty-two, i have been badly hurt. i see her, little mouth,

bare-faced & vulnerable. i see her & don't know where to begin.

1,000

My roommate one year in college
would say of my smallness
that any man who found me attractive
had a trace of the pedophilic

& I would shrink, newly girled
twenty-one with my eyebrows plucked
to grownup arches, sprouting back
every three weeks in sharp little shoots.

Already men have tried to steal me
in their taxis, corral me into alleyways
of the new city. Already the demand for my name
though no one ever asks how old I am,

though no one ever did. I feel creaking
& ancient in the repetition of it all.
I feel my girlhood gone for generations
my entire line of blood crowded

with exhausted women.
Their unlined faces frozen in time
with only a thickness about the waist,
a small shoot of gray to belie the years.

I make up names to hand to strangers at parties.
I trim years from my age & share
without being asked, that I am fifteen,
seventeen, & no one blinks.
No one stops wanting.

I am disappeared like all the girls
before me, around me,
all the girls to come.

Everyone thinks I am a little girl
& still they hunt me, still they show their teeth.
I am so tired, I am one thousand years old.
One thousand years older when touched.

SUMMER TRIANGLE

say i formed a body of clay around
a clot of dried blood
i formed a body of dirt & water
i formed a body of water around red earth & cracked clay
i formed a body polluted by want
most of it not mine

i formed a body purified by name
washed in the white water of my grandfather's blind left eye
washed with my grandmother's feet in ablution

i formed a body to be left behind
to be unzipped & discarded
to return to perfumed aunts
arranged in jagged sleep
waking only to tie systems of jasmine into my torn hair

i formed a body suspended in utterance
named & undone & named again

girl   lacuna   specter   throat
throat [say it] *bloodstain   sheet*   [name it]

i formed a body darkened by blood
the moon tugging its irons from my shameful parts

i formed a body & swam
inelegant laps in rising water
temperate as the first womb

& always ships darkening the banks like blood
& always water dividing the world
god's country clotting out between my legs like silk

PALIMPSEST

i wear the dead girl's clothes

all my adornments pulled from the bodies of animals

ambergris & musk & tallow

i smell it in my hair

i stink of my every mother

my fingernails bright & rotted in henna

my fingernails kneading raw lamb & dried onion

i wear the white & mourn

i wear the amulets bound in leather

i write it down

to dissolve into water & drink

i did not stand bare before a mirror

i did not invite the eye

i did not surrender to the drum

beaten to pull dark spirits from the bodies of women

mesmeric dance

mesmeric twist of the cigarette smoke

i did not smoke

i burned the sandalwood & recited

i burned the sandalwood & memorized

i waited in the dark for something to fetch me

HARDER/BORDER

my each & every name   my casing   a border
my body my mouth my failing tongue   a border

my grandfather   milk pooling in his hopeful eye
[say it]   i lost a language & grew another border

spoiled milk   my curdling citizenship   my liquid
spilling citizenship   my missing names a border

poured everywhere & drying in the yellow morning
my body is touched & i claw the air for my borders

i misplace my homeland   mispronounce my mother
tongue   [again]   [louder]   [harder]   [border]

imagine my mirror mouth   its boundless dark   all
my alternate selves better   broader   bolder   border

louder   thinner   [say it]   though purity is [i know]
an invention   she bleeds blacker brimming   border

my grandfather's girl   matching milk   [صافية]   pure
citizened & born backward   imagine me softer   border

ODE TO GOSSIPS

i was mothered by lonely women
some of them wives

some of them with plumes of smoke for husbands
all lonely

smelling of onions & milk
all mothers

some of them to children
some to old names

phantom girls acting out a life
only half a life away

instead they clatter copper kitchenware
with their bangles pushed up the arm

their fingernails rusted with henna
& kneading raw lamb with salt
with coriander

they take weak tea
upper lip sweating in the steam
hair unwound against the nape

my deities   each one
each sandal slapping against each stone heel
their funk of sandalwood & oud

i worship the bright chiffon
spun about each head
the coffee in the dowry china
the butter biscuits on a painted plate
crumbs suspended in eggshell demitasse
when they begin:

i heard   *people are saying*
        i saw it with my own eyes

[   ]'s daughter   *a scandal*
she was wearing [   ]   & not wearing [   ]

                can you imagine?

a shame   *a shame*

GIRLS THAT NEVER DIE

i cover my shoulders in a photograph so the hissing will quiet
i cloister my vices
    i maintain my weight
      i never cut my hair

i am asked to change my dress
i am asked to line my eyes
never an order only the slight apology
    [people will talk]

i am asked to take down the photo
    i am asked to anonymize my lover

stop showing my teeth
    cover my knees
      shave my legs
        stop wearing red
          start wearing makeup
          stop wearing lipstick

stop being photographed at night

    people will talk
    what will they think?
    what will they do with my name?

∴

بنت ناس /bint nas/ *n.* daughter of People; girl with a Name;
unbroken yolk as reputation; daily maintenance of Name; girlhood
governed by Tongues; reputation as system of value; virgin; sane;
oiled & brushed; fluent; chaste & shy; reputation as condition for
Name; reputation as condition for daughterhood; reputation-
shaped urn;

                             ;name;

∴

They cut the hair of disgraced girls so I cut it myself.

Took the razor to it myself. I wanted to feel the bone, its hardness,

untouched skin against its newborn curve. & thereby purified

I slept, only to wake the next morning to it returned, the same

puffed braid I wore throughout my girlhood. The baby hairs

brushed down with cream. Two thick elastics like the knotted ends

of sausage. & again in the mirror I made the cuts, fat tufts drifting

like feathers to carpet the cold tile. I walked everywhere with scissors,

left hair on buses & at parties, cursive scrawls in other beds, handed it

in fistfuls, stuffed in pillowcases. Whole braids still bound with their elastic,

curled in commas on the pavement behind me, scattered like acacia pods,

my ellipsis, my thousand confessions.

∴

i was twenty-four & almost died & nobody knew
i was [fourteen][sixteen][twenty] & nobody knew
   i was sick in my heart in my blood i fainted the train
   i was [   ] i fainted the [man]
started moving i started to empty from my body while it fell
started moving i started to empty from my body while it fell
   everything suspended & viscous i fell very slowly
   everything suspended & viscous i fell very slowly
i had time to name it before a stranger caught my weight
i [could not] name it [& keep my name] a stranger [   ]

& later i kept quiet told no one i knew what they would think

& later i kept quiet told no one i knew what they would think

i knew what could be said i knew what stories form

i knew what could be said i knew what stories form

    when bodies float into the tracks before trains   i fell

    when bodies [   ] [   ] [   ] [   ]   i [   ]

& was caught & the next day brushed my hair & dressed

& was [not] caught & the next day brushed my hair & dressed

    loosely & chastely & went on hollowing all mouths of my name

    loosely & chastely & went on hollowing all mouths of my name

..

i obeyed & still

i covered & still

i prayed & still

i stayed home & still

i dressed loosely & still

i plaited my hair & still

i was unpainted & still

i was a child & still

i was an adult & still

i moved cities & still

i lived with roommates & still

i lowered my eyes & still

i cut my hair & still

i was polite & still

i was silent & still

i was alone once

i was lonely

it was dark

it was daylight

i was a girl & like the girls i knew

i bruised i bled i died

∴

سُمْعَة /sum·'a/ *n.* reputation; shared root with سمع /su·mi·'a/ *n.*
hearing; as in; i heard that man's daughter was seen [   ] while
wearing [   ] such a shame with that complexion that hair she
could have been [   ]; i heard that man's daughter smokes
cigarettes & opens her mouth to laugh such a shame she must not
have a father; i heard that man's daughter is no longer that man's
daughter & cannot close her legs; i heard that man's daughter lost
her People lost her surname when she lost her [   ]; i heard
that man's daughter was never a daughter has no People has no
reputation has no Name;

∴

what small freedoms could i exchange for my name for my Name

for the sound people make when they daughter me for my cage for my

سمعة for what people hear in the absence of my cloistered body for the

sentencing after [i heard] for the sentences locked away before my name

my Name pries itself open my name my Name prized above my body above

my mouth my name shrouds my body magnifies its every act my cage

my Name my cage my reputation my unbroken yolk my unstained sheet

my cage my stage my blood my sheet my

∴

But what if I will not die?

What will govern me then?

How to govern me then?

What bounty, then, on my name?

What stone   What rope   What man

will be my officer?

FOR MY FRIENDS,
IN REPLY TO A QUESTION

I'm okay. And, of course, I'm not,
but I go through the motions. I wake up
to the alarm's howl, even when the word
in my body is *no*. I dress in livid colors.
I blacken the hairs of each eyebrow. I bake
& braise & pickle. I write & read & lose
hours to the blur of the television. I sit
for hours in the bath, my skin puckering.
I don't know if I'll ever go home again.
I don't know who I've seen for the last time.
The Arabic comes back to me in streaks
of paint, verb forms & vocabularies
I may never again have occasion to use.
My days smudge into one another & it's not
that I am afraid. It's as if I am watching it
all happen below, & I am somewhere above
the room, wondering if the rice is burning.

I am somewhere above the room, watching
my new aches, watching the news as if
I am reading it in a novel. I look up
the names of people I knew in childhood,
learn their new & angular faces, their
faraway lives. My grandfather pixelates
into a smile & I work my creaking muscles
to replicate it. I do not ask if we will ever
meet again, I do not ask him to read to me,
or for anything that will make me long.
I dull it with sugar & oil, with cooking shows,
with sleep. I sleep twelve hours each night
& in my dreams I am fleeing a war, in my dreams
I am touching the faces of my friends, we are
each one of us touching, & even in the dream
we are afraid.

RED NOTE WITH A LINE
BY OL' DIRTY BASTARD

If you read this in red don't think I didn't survive. Every day I go
missing: One eyelash at a time or sometimes all at once. & in the
absence of disgrace I walk in & out of rivers & wear my good silk.
My good clean unburnt body dripping in the honey light. I sprout
leaves. I bear fruit & self-sustain. I tread water. I flake the moon for
my boundless hair & another grows in its place. I am sistered but
never again to a dead girl. Nowhere, ever again, is there a dead girl.
Somewhere our wounds seal; our stitches fall away. Somewhere a
rope turns & our feet never touch the ground. Somewhere a song
plays & names us with each touch of a needle to the shining surface
of its black: *I'm hanging out /partying / with girls / that never die*

GIRLS THAT NEVER DIE

a girl   buried
to the chest in red earth   her wrists

bound beneath the soil
with twine   a crowd gathers

to father her   its infinite
hands   curved loosely around

a stone   small enough
that no single throw   is named

as cause of death   no single
hand   accountable to the blood

a girl   undaughter   unnamed
unfaced   undone from the lineage

her photographs   pulled already
from bookshelf   from walls   a father

among the hands   his pebble
streaked with quartz   the first to rise

to carve the air & arc   toward the girl
the rootless tree   faceless & erect

& perhaps the stones   twisting
like fireworks   the girl

their nucleus   rise   & rise
for a time   opposite of rain

opposite of hail & perhaps the silence
a beat too long   & another

another   & then a rustling
of wings   above the girl

a flock   thick mixed cloud
of avifauna   partridge & nightjar

& golden sparrow   & avocet
& lapwing   & every other sort

of plover   & ibis & heron & gulls
though the sea   is far & to the north

& the minutes pass & the girl is untouched
& each bird in its beak   tongues a stone

NOTES

FINAL WEEKS, 1990

This poem was written in response to a prompt from Louise Glück to write a poem that takes place the day you were born, in which both the time of year and time of day must be clear. The final line is after a line by Warsan Shire: "I have my mother's mouth and my father's eyes; on my face they are still together."

ORPHEUS

This poem is built of scraps of poems written during a 30/30 in August 2020 with Hala Alyan, so while these poems are not "after" poems of hers in the conventional sense, I believe them to be shaped by the presence of her poems in my inbox during the time of their writing.

PROFANITY

The first section of this poem is published in *POETRY* as "self-portrait with profanity." The second half is published in *FUSION* as "ode to swearing."

HOW TO SAY

This poem is written after Agha Shahid Ali's poem "In Arabic" and originally appears in the Academy of American Poets' *Poem-a-Day*.

YASMEEN

This poem originally appears in *POETRY*. This poem was also the kernel of an idea that later became the novel-in-verse *Home Is Not a Country*. I found Tyehimba Jess's book *Olio* incredibly instructive when I was working with the contrapuntal form.

TAXONOMY [*I GO TO MEET THE POEM . . .*]

This poem originally appears in *Pleiades*. The line "family honor is in the body of the girl" is based on a quote from an anonymous source in the *Vanity Fair* article *"You're Essentially a Prisoner": Why Do Dubai's Princesses Keep Trying to Escape?* by Vanessa Grigoriadis. The original quote is "family honor is within the girl—her virginity is the family's honor."

INFIBULATION STUDY [*I WILL BEGIN BY WRITING A SENTENCE . . .*]

The first draft of this poem was based on a drama therapy intervention called "doubling," where the therapist listens to a client tell a story, then repeats back an interpretation of parts of the story, followed by "if this is true, repeat it, if it is not, correct it."

POMEGRANATE WITH PARTIAL NUDE

This poem bases its title on what I think is the title of a painting called "Pomegranate with Female Nude" that I thought I saw in a book about Salvador Dalí once and wrote it down, but now I can't find it. I wrote this while listening to the song "Ph City Vibration" by Burna Boy, and the lyric "south side of the river of the garden city" found its way into the poem as the lines "seven countries from my garden city" and "sun sets on the pomegranate city."

INFIBULATION STUDY [*WHAT IS TO BORDER BUT TO CUT . . .*]

This poem originally appears in *Gulf Coast*.

ISHA, NEW YORK CITY

A version of this poem appears in the chapbook *ars poetica* (MIEL, 2016).

MEMOIR

The first draft of this poem was also written during that summer 2020 30/30 with Hala.

[*DON'T EVER GO INTO A ROOM ALONE WITH ANYONE . . .*]

This one too (the 30/30).

ON EID WE SLAUGHTER LAMBS & I KNOW INTIMATELY THE COLOR

This poem originally appears in the *Missing Slate*.

A RUMOR

This poem originally appears in *Barrelhouse* and was written at Cave Canem.

MODERN SUDANESE POETRY

This poem originally appears in *POETRY* and borrows its title from the anthology *Modern Sudanese Poetry* (University of Nebraska Press, 2019). It also appears in the *PANK* folio *Azza fi Hawak: a Collection of Sudanese Poetry.*

GIRLS THAT NEVER DIE [*A GIRL   EMBROIDERED . . .*]

This poem originally appears in *Barrelhouse* and was the first poem I wrote under this title.

SELF-PORTRAIT WITHOUT STITCHES

This poem is written after Tarfia Faizullah's "100 Bells" and originally appears in the *Poetry Review.*

THE ANIMAL

This poem originally appears in *American Poetry Review.*

THE CAIRO APARTMENTS

This poem originally appears in *The Atlantic* and was written in response to an assignment from Louise Glück to write a prose poem that uses conventional capitalization and punctuation.

ZAMALEK

This poem is written after Kim Addonizio's "New Year's Day." Another August 2020 30/30 poem.

GENEVA

This poem originally appears in the *Columbia Review*. 30/30.

TONY SOPRANO'S TENDER MACHISMO

Yet another August 30/30 poem, written after watching *The Sopranos* for the first time.

SUMMER

30/30!

TAXONOMY [*WANTING WAS MY LANGUAGE FIRST . . .*]

An early draft of this poem was written as a commission for the program book for three works of Wayne McGregor's that premiered at the Bavarian State Ballet in 2018. The poem was particularly inspired by the piece "Borderlands."

SYROS

This poem is written after Jenny Xie's poem "Corfu" and originally appears in the *Columbia Review*.

TERRA NULLIUS

This poem was written in response to another prompt from Louise Glück which, among other elements, required the word "then" to appear five times in the poem.

TAXONOMY [*BECAUSE I CANNOT FIND THE WORDS . . .*]

This poem was written while spending a lot of time with Ladan Osman's poem "Trouble."

BORDER/SOFTER

A version of this poem appears in the *Progressive* and the section in italics refers to "Winston's Hiccup"—"after a particularly liquid lunch, Churchill was said to have created Transjordan with a stroke of his pen."

ODE TO MY HOMEGIRLS

This poem originally appears in *BOMB* and is written after Matthew Olzmann's poem "Mountain Dew Commercial Disguised as a Love Poem."

GIRLS THAT NEVER DIE [*PERHAPS A COW . . .*]

This poem originally appears in *POETRY.*

ELEGY

Another August 2020 30/30 poem!

1,000

A version of this poem appears in the Academy of American Poets'
Poem-a-day.

SUMMER TRIANGLE

The first draft of this poem was written in response to a piece by
Laura Christensen, originally by the same title and since renamed
"To Dwell Midst the Waves," as a commission for Laura's book
"THEN AGAIN: Vintage Photography Reimagined by One Artist
and Thirty-One Writers."

HARDER/BORDER

This poem was commissioned by and originally appears in *Art Papers*.

ODE TO GOSSIPS

An earlier version of this poem appears in *POETRY*.

GIRLS THAT NEVER DIE [*I COVER MY SHOULDERS . . .*]

The third section of this poem originally appears in *Ambit*. The last
section of this poem originally appears in *POETRY*.

FOR MY FRIENDS, IN REPLY TO A QUESTION

This poem is written after David Ignatow's poem "For My Daughter, in Reply to a Question" and appears in *Catapult*.

RED NOTE WITH A LINE BY OL' DIRTY BASTARD

This poem is written after Danez Smith's poem "summer, some-where" and originally appears under the title "after" in *West Branch*, as well as in the anthology *Women of Resistance: Poems for a New Feminism*. It borrows the line "I'm hanging out/partying/with girls/ that never die" from Ol' Dirty Bastard's verse on the song "Ghetto Supastar" by Pras featuring ODB and Mya.

GIRLS THAT NEVER DIE *[A GIRL   BURIED . . .]*

This poem originally appears in *POETRY*.

ACKNOWLEDGMENTS

This is the book I was most afraid to write. I am so grateful to my communities for holding me and caring for me and keeping me safe during this work. To my sisters, my siblings, breaking free of that long silence. Thank you for trusting me with your stories. Thank you for hearing mine.

Thank you to Nicole Counts, my editor, for your tender attention, for seeing the book inside this book so many drafts ago. Thank you to Kwame Dawes, most trusted caretaker of my poems, for your guidance and your rigor (and for putting this book in its correct order). Thank you to the team at One World for giving this book a dream home, and to Tabia Yapp for helping me wish this life into existence.

Thank you to my teachers, to the classrooms of your living rooms and text threads and emails and coffee shops and phone calls and workshop spaces. Thank you to Louise Glück, under whose mentorship my poems grew up and began to assert themselves, to punctuate themselves, to speak clearly. Thank you to Kamau Brathwaite and Eavan Boland. I am grateful my time in this world overlapped with yours. Thank you to the homies who underwent several rounds of manuscript boot camp with me, over several years, to get this incredibly unruly manuscript under control: Fatimah Asghar, Hieu Minh Nguyen, Justin Phillip Reed, Donovan Ramsey, Jay Ellis. Thank you to my homies who are my home teams, Team Mashallah (Angel, Hanif, Kaveh, Fati) and Team Cowork (Liz, Clint). Thank you to Camonghne Felix, for your sisterhood, for everything you've taught me to do. Thank you to Alison Rollins for our Monday exchanges. Thank you to Hala Alyan for inviting me to write 31 poems in the 31 days of August 2020 together—my love of your work made my poems better, imagining you reading them on the other end. So many of those poems found their way into this book, and shaped it. Thank you to my Stegner cohort, to my Beotis family, to the communities that nurtured and raised me: Cave Canem, the DC Youth Slam Team, Slam! at NYU, and Split This Rock.

I was given the gift of space and time to draft and revise these poems, and that gift made this book possible. Thank you to the Wallace Stegner fellowship at Stanford, and to the residencies at Troutbeck and SPACE on Ryder Farm and Cave Canem. In your care I relearned to write poems, and found my way into this book.

To my family, my families, I am so lucky to be your girl. Safaa El-Kogali, I am so lucky to be your daughter. Almustafa Elhillo, I am so lucky to be your sister. Habab Elmahdi and Eltayeb El-Kogali, I am so lucky to be your granddaughter. To my cousins and aunties and uncles and nieces and nephews, thank you, I love you. To everyone who came before: I will spend the rest of my life making sure I know your names. To Awrad and Basma: Most of these poems were texts between us first. Thank you for making me brave, for keeping me safe, for our 20 years and counting. I am so lucky to be married to Christopher Gabriel Núñez, who every day makes me a life I love, makes me laugh, makes breakfast. You are number one, very best. Thank you to Margarita and Fernando and Karina and Tatiana and JP and Tía Olga and Tía Fanny for welcoming me, for loving me back.

I don't know how to end this. I can't believe this book is finished. I can't believe it's going to be in the world. Thank you for reading it. Thank you for hearing me out.

ABOUT THE AUTHOR

Sudanese by way of D.C., SAFIA ELHILLO is the author of *The January Children* and *Home Is Not a Country* and co-editor of the anthology *Halal If You Hear Me*. Winner of the Sillerman First Book Prize for African Poets, the Arab American Book Award, and the Brunel International African Poetry Prize, she is also the recipient of a Cave Canem Fellowship and a Ruth Lilly and Dorothy Sargent Rosenberg Fellowship from the Poetry Foundation. Her work has appeared in *POETRY* magazine, *Callaloo*, and the Academy of American Poets' Poem-a-day series, among others. Currently a Wallace Stegner Fellow at Stanford University, she lives in Oakland, California.

safia-mafia.com
Twitter: mafiasafia
Instagram: safiamafia

ABOUT THE TYPE

This book was set in Bembo, a typeface based on an old-style Roman face that was used for Cardinal) Pietro Bembo's tract De Aetna in 1495. Bembo was cut by Francesco Griffo (1450–1518) in the early sixteenth century for Italian Renaissance printer and publisher Aldus Manutius (1449–1515). The Lanston Monotype Company of Philadelphia brought the well-proportioned letterforms of Bembo to the United States in the 1930s.